THE ART OF
ANGELS &
CHERUBS

Miranda Fellows

A Compilation of Works from the
BRIDGEMAN ART LIBRARY

Angels and Cherubs

This edition first published in Great Britain in 1995
by Parragon Book Service Limited

© 1995 Parragon Book Service Limited

ISBN 0-7525-0805-9

Printed in Italy

ANGELS AND CHERUBS

It is hard to imagine believing that angels ruled the universe, that they controlled gravity, could move stars and moons, that they could guard and protect us, or trick and deceive us. But there was a time when people thought it so, and described visitations by these celestial beings in elaborate words and vivid images. We have inherited this artistic legacy, one full of contradictions and repetitions, myth and magic. Following the path which angels have travelled is difficult yet rewarding, taking us on many rich diversions along the way.

The word 'angel' gives us a clue to its meaning. Derived from the Greek *angelos*, it meant 'shadow side of God', 'messenger' or 'revealer of truth'. Born before humans, angels are superior to them in intelligence and status. Angels were given free will by God – those who chose good were given a state of eternal grace, those who chose evil found themselves cast out of heaven into Hell. Angels have appeared in many religions, philosophies as well as in classical mythology.

To make the sense of all this clearer, we should consider the hierarchy to which angels are said to adhere. Although there are discrepancies between the theories pronounced, the general belief seems to be that angels exist within three heavenly zones.

In the highest reside Seraphim, Cherubim and Thrones. They are in direct communication with God. Cherubim have a single pair of blue wings, are often dressed in bishop's robes and are the relaters of knowledge. Seraphim have three pairs of red wings, four heads and carry flame-like swords. They emanate divine love. The Thrones are multi-eyed chariots or wheels which transport God's message. These angels are never in direct communication with humanity – they pass God's word to the second level, to the Powers and Virtues.

The Dominions, or Powers and Virtues, are the managers of all of the angels in heaven, and they guard the pearly gates. They communicate all messages from the first triad to the third, are hugely courageous and are often called brilliant or shining, like stars. They adhere to many a description of heavenly angels in their whiteness, brighter than any white known on earth. They can be good or evil, however, and one of their jobs is said to be the balancing of souls – the attempt to reconcile good and evil within humankind. These angels are said to be ruled by the Archangels, who exist in the third triad with the multitude of angels who filter God's messages down to humanity.

Who the Archangels actually are is hard to define, but for our purpose only six are really important – Gabriel, Michael, Metatron, Raphael, Uriel and Satanel, all of whom make regular appearance in Western art.

Metatron is often cited as the most important Archangel, the closest to God and the King of Angels, and one who seems to exist within many guises.

Michael himself is a far more substantial character than Metraton. As ruler of Israel, he is protector of God's Holy Land. He is also the judge of souls and leads them into heaven. He is said to have led the war against Satan when he rebelled in the Kingdom of Heaven, and is God's personal bodyguard.

Michael's most startling characteristics are visual ones, making him a favourite subject for painters of religious scenes. He is always ready for battle, so often appears in soldier's armour. His wings are significant in that they are made from peacock feathers. This has created many a myth.

Gabriel is the only archangel often depicted as a female. Gabriel was first mentioned 500 years before Michael and she is as central to Islam as to Christianity. She told Daniel of the coming of the Messiah, Zacharias of the arrival of St John the Baptist. When she appeared before Mohammed and revealed the Koran her wings stretched from east to west across the world. Most importantly to Christians, Gabriel told Mary of the Annunciation. Gabriel has saffron hair, yellow feet and jade green wings. She is often adorned with rubies and coral. In Islam the words, 'There is no God but God, and Mohammed is the Prophet of God' are emblazoned between her eyes. Often the easiest way to spot the Archangel Gabriel in religious art is to look for the white lily – the angel holding it will be her. It is the symbol of perpetual purity.

chastity and grace and she gave it to Mary at the Annunciation.

Archangel Raphael is the healer of humans and the doctor of the angels. He guards the Tree of Life and is usually shown with six wings.

We know what Satan symbolizes, but it is worth considering that he was not always a rebel angel and that he did have a role to play in Heaven before he incited revolt. If angels are like Satan, they are capable of evil.

As well as the Archangels, the third triad also contains the angels who communicate directly with humans. They are most human in their appearance and are vulnerable to misadventure.

The final angel we must mention is also the most chilling: the Angel of Death, who draws the soul out and steals it away. He is called Azrael. In classical mythology he has four faces and four pairs of wings, and his body is covered with eyes. It is said that when one blinks, a soul dies.

In painting, the characteristics of all of these angels are not always reproduced as described above. Cultural and social context and the change in artistic intentions over the centuries have affected the way in which angels have been depicted.

Cherubs are a classic example of this change. Originally they were seen as terrifying creatures – vile in appearance with many heads and bodies – who stood at the entrance to Paradise and guarded celestial palaces and kingdoms. But as time has passed their appearance has altered and become fixed in its Renaissance state, that of curly-haired babies with wings, musical instruments, the occasional bow and arrow. About the only suggestion of their more formidable past is apparent in their sometimes devilish expressions.

There was a time when the depiction of an angel was laden with meaning, its appearance in the stained glass of a church apse or on the frescoed ceiling of a palace or monastery protecting those who entered within. Now we admire them more for their decorative characteristics. Within these pages perhaps we may learn also to understand the subtleties which existed between them – and just what each artist, in his or her own personal way, was trying to tell us about the world they inhabited.

◁ **Mural from the Tomb of San Pablo de Casserres**
(detail showing angels with trumpets from the Last Judgement)
13th century
Pablo de Casserres

Fresco

THIS HEAVILY stylized and decorative painting of angels is characteristic of the Romanesque period when it was painted. Unlike later depictions of angels, which make them appear as human as possible, in Romanesque painting it was more common to depict them as decorative symbols. The shape of the body and the angle of the head are repeated from the first angel to the second to create pattern and rhythm. Their wings envelop them and they are crowned by halos – a characteristic not always adhered to in later examples.

◁ **Angels from the Lamentation** c 1305
Ambrogio Bondone Giotto
(1266/7-1337)

Fresco

GIOTTO, FAMED FOR developing
the basic principles of modern
western art, here explores his new
found skill at creating depth and
perspective on the picture surface.
These angels tumble happily
through the illusion of space.
Although they have human heads,
wings are attached to their bodies,
emphasizing that they are not
human forms. It was commonly
held at this time that angels had
no forewarning of Christ's
incarnation, passion or
resurrection, so that all His
experiences were as startling and
unexpected to them as to
humanity. They differed from
humans in their unbending faith
in all that He stood for and did.

◁ **The Annunciation** c 1436
(detail showing the Angel Gabriel, with St Peter the Martyr behind)
Fra Angelico c 1400-55

Fresco

AS SERMONS, Fra Angelico's paintings were simple and instructive rather than elaborate and mystical. He was influenced by Giotto and the Gothic style, and had a clear grasp of the laws of perspective. Gabriel is simply garmented, his hair characteristically blonde and styled in tight curls. He does not hold lilies and gives no outward sign of his purpose in coming to see Mary. His is a serene, classical poise, his halo and hidden feet adding to the sense of his lightness, enhanced by his wings. It is worth noting that in this image of the Annunciation, Gabriel is adorned in identical robes and with the same wings as in another Annunciation scene by Fra Angelica which hangs in Museo di San Marco, Florence.

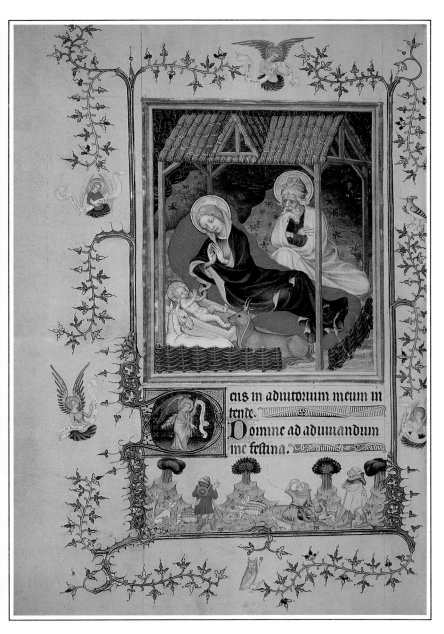

◁ The Nativity: Visitation of the Shepherds

from the Duc de Berry's *Très Belle Heures* c 1400–7

IT IS INTERESTING to see angels being used to decorate the border of an illuminated manuscript. They are separated from the main image of Mary, Joseph and Jesus by a frame, and from the shepherds and their flocks below by a golden bough. They come bearing the message of God on scrolls and are attached to the Tree of Life. As was common in early iconography, the angels and the shepherds are depicted as far smaller figures than the family, who are of central interest to the narrative. But the angels are celestial, and as such are separated from the shepherds by a second frame, to suggest their different realms. Their existence in the air rather than on earth is emphasized by the images of birds. Note how one cherubim, wings fiery red, is used as a purely decorative choice, sitting within the first calligraphic letter of the scriptures.

Detail

◁ **The Seven Sacraments** *(central panel of triptych)*
Roger van der Weyden (1399–1464)

Oil on canvas

VAN DER WEYDEN was one of the most highly regarded artists in Flanders in the 15th century, famed for his fine detail, humanism and high spiritualism. He tended to use brighter colours than his contemporaries: the white, yellow and red gowns of these angels are characteristic choices. He also concentrated on creating depth on the canvas, as is readily apparent here. The angels bear their messages on scrolls for the audience below to read: a common method used by artists to show angels presenting the word of God.

Detail

▷ **Madonna and Child Surrounded by Eight Angels** 1453-55
Marco Zoppo (1433-78)

Tempera on panel

THE CHERUBS which surround the Madonna and Child do not appear to be providing her with any messages from God, or giving guardianship against intrusion. Instead, they appear as churlish infants, more intent upon their own playful pursuits than her well-being! Here we have the classic early Renaissance emergence of the curly-haired cherub. They are a noisy bunch, playing musical instruments and twisting and turning around her. Their role is as decorative as it is narrative, they help create a frame around the mother and child. Their wings have become tiny, their halos have gone. Their spiritual significance has been lessened in favour of the artist's humanist depiction.

Detail

▷ **The Three Angels and Tobias**
Francesco Botticini (1446-97)

NOT RECOGNIZED for his individuality of style, Botticini nevertheless learned much from his mentors, who included Botticelli and Filipino Lippi. This painting demonstrates how he would use artistic licence in the creation of a scene. Tobias was met by the Archangel Raphael alone, but here, for want, we presume, of further decoration, he has been joined by fellow angels Gabriel and Michael. But Raphael seems to sport Michael's peacock wings, presumably in an attempt to embellish him further. Michael, to the left, carries his unsheathed sword, and Gabriel, to the right, the characteristic lily, symbol of chastity.

Detail

◁ **The Annunciation** *(detail)*
Filippino Lippi (1457/8-1504)

Fresco

LIPPI WAS FORTUNATE to be Botticelli's assistant and from him he learned to articulate line and colour with an unusual deftness and skill. This Annunciation scene demonstrates the master's skill of rendering. Note how it is now Gabriel who is fortunate enough to have peacock feather wings, and how the flowers in his hair, crown a bent and modest head. The origin of the lily, symbol of chastity and purity, is said to be the Garden of Eden. When Eve was expelled, it is said that she cried tears which fell to the ground and grew into lilies.

◁ **Putto with Festoon**
(fresco fragment)
Raphael Sanzio of Urbino
(1483-1520)

Fresco

THE SIMPLE, perfect face and
form of the putto (cherub) is
reflective of Raphael's fluency as a
High Renaissance master. The
innocent eyes and freshness of the
flesh, combined with the
contrapposto of the body and the
naturalistic golden locks, are a
celebration of his simple yet
perfectly balanced style. The
cherub does not have any wings to
speak of in this image. High
Renaissance painters often
omitted halos and wings for the
sake of balance and harmony.

▷ The Sistine Madonna
Raphael Sanzio of Urbino
(1483-1520)

THE SISTINE MADONNA is one of
the few works by Raphael which
is said to have been executed
entirely by the master's own hand.
Considering how busy he was
with commissions, the reason why
he spent so much time on it is a
matter for conjecture. The
cherubs emphasize the heavenly
state within which Raphael has
placed the Madonna. Her image
has come a long way from early
depictions of her as a normal
peasant girl endowed with the
greatest gift from God. Here, she
is Mother of God, raised
triumphantly on high. The image
is simple and light, the two
cherubs adding a touch of
humour to an otherwise austere
religious scene.

Detail

▷ **Madonna and Child with St John the Baptist**
Giovanni Battista (Fiorentino) Rosso (1494-1540)

Oil on canvas

IN THIS LATE Renaissance painting, it is not the cherubs who have halos but the Madonna, Christ and John the Baptist. They add decoration and a reflection, perhaps, of the youthfulness of the boy Christ. One of the founding artists of Mannerism, this work still shows all of the signs of a classical training, yet with the beginnings of an expressionism showing in the faces of the figures.

Detail

◁ **The Dead Christ Supported by an Angel**
Antonello da Messina (1430-79)

THE MOTIF of angels supporting Christ was first introduced by Donatello, but re-emerged in the hand of Zoppo, Crivelli, Bellini, and as we see here, Messina. The single angel expresses Christ's agony by his downcast eyes and mouth, in contrast to Christ's head which is tilted heavenward in its mortal pain. The skull by the angel's foot represents Christ's imminent Ascension, and by holding onto him from behind, the angel is supporting his soul. The narrative is set against a classical backdrop, a tableau of the countryside, strewn with further skulls and bones.

◁ **Pieta**
Antonello da Messina (1430-79)

AGAIN, MESSINA concentrates on the image of Christ being supported by angels, but here, unlike in the previous example, there are three. The image is far less detailed and more muted in tone than before. Christ's head is hung low and the three angels support and surround him, their wings suggesting the journey he is about to take upwards to Heaven. The positioning of Christ renders him leaden in weight and the angels really appear to be straining to support him. Again, skulls and bones strew the distant landscape.

◁ **Archangel Gabriel**
Sandro Botticelli (1444/5-1510)

Fresco

BOTTICELLI'S DEPICTION of the
Archangel Gabriel descending to
tell Mary of her expected child is
a mastery of grace and gesture,
fine line and intricate detail.
Gabriel is seen dramatically
floating in his flowing garments,
his hair a wave of saffron curls, his
wings glorious and golden. And
from his crown sprouts his symbol
of chastity – the lily flower. He is
an arresting figure. In this
painting it is easy to see why the
Pre-Raphaelites so admired
Botticelli's classical style.

Detail

▷ **Vallombrosa altarpiece** *(detail of angel musicians)*
Pietro Perugino (1445-1523)

THE CLARITY of Perugino's design was much celebrated in his lifetime and it is widely believed that he helped pave the way towards the High Renaissance with his clarity, balance and ordered compositions. It is interesting to see an image in which the angels are not all depicted as human forms with wings. Although the cherubs have baby faces, they have no bodies. As St Thomas Aquinas had deduced that angels were pure intelligences, not united bodies, and as intelligence lies in the head, this was the most important part. The more human angel musicians come from the lowest triad and their music would be used to pass on the messages of the cherubs, who had heard them direct from God. They would have believed that music would help relay their messages to man more clearly. The angel at the bottom of the composition appears to be carrying a child – perhaps she is a symbol for the Virgin mother.

The Annunciation
Leonardo da Vinci (1452-1519)

Oil and tempera on a wood panel

▷ *Overleaf pages 30-31*

ONLY FORMALLY attributed to Leonardo in 1939, this is an early work and is far more stylized and less confident than later paintings. The outdoor setting is unusual for Leonardo, but the walled garden is said to symbolize virginity, as does the lily. In contrast to earlier artists' interpretations of the angel, which tend to give him superhuman qualities, Leonardo's Gabriel is distinctly human, if androgynous in appearance, denoting the new concentration on humanism in religious iconography. His wings are carefully contrived to appear bird-like and natural. There are several examples of angels in Leonardo's work, but during this period their popularity was waning, due to overexposure in religious painting of the Renaissance.

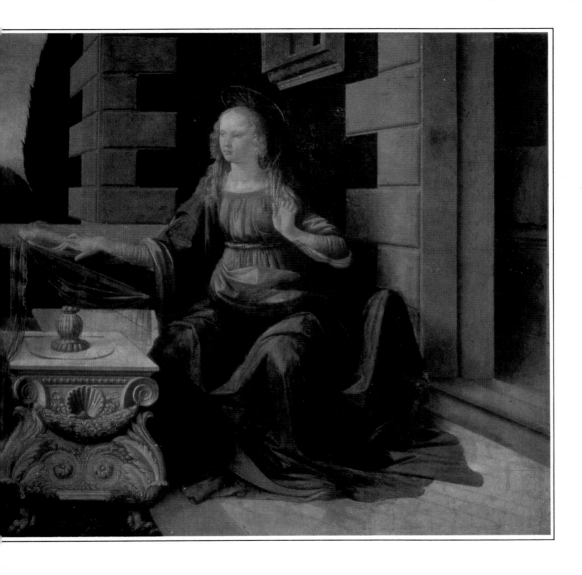

▷ The Mystic Nativity
Sandro Botticelli (1444/5-1510)

Oil on canvas

BOTTICELLI'S SCENE celebrates the birth of Christ and the triumph of good over the evil of Satan's reign on earth. The Nativity story is taken from St Luke's Gospel, Chapter 2, where the birth of Christ marks the beginning of a reign of peace. All of the angels are carrying olive branches, as a sign of this new-found utopia. Those above the stable are dancing in celebration, those in the middle are leading the shepherds to Christ and the three in the foreground are embracing man at this moment of reconciliation. Note how the devils are writhing in agony on the ground at their loss of power.

△ Angel Playing the Lute
Giovanni Battista (Fiorentino) Rosso (1494-1540)

Oil on canvas

THERE IS A SOFT, surreal quality to this painting, common to the work of Rosso. The figure is emotive and sensual, the setting is irrelevant, the sheer pleasure that the angel gains in playing his musical instrument is of central importance to the image. The angel of music is generally accepted as being Uriel, and this was probably meant to be one of his choir rather than himself. Music was believed to be the angelic art – deriving from the heavens and raising people into a spiritual consciousness unlike their day-to-day experience. It was also believed that music aided us in our understanding of the higher language of the celestial beings.

Detail

▷ **Madonna and Child**
David Gerard (1460-1523)

Oil on canvas

VAN DER WEYDEN and Memlinc are the unquestioned influences on this artist of the Netherlands. The angels are used as a decorative device to crown the Madonna and give her a spiritual dimension. They are typically northern in their appearance. It was common for artists of the 15th century to paint angels with distinctly human qualities, with wings but no halos. They were usually reduced in size to differentiate them from the human species. Note the elaborate detailing Gerard has created in the crown, ensuring the superiority of the Madonna.

◁ **Child Angel Playing a Flute** c 1500
Bernardino Luini (1480-1532)

DURING HIS LIFETIME, such images as this Child Angel gained Luini great popularity in his home town of Milan. An avid follower of Leonardo da Vinci, one can see how he took his mentor's example to the extreme – the image is slightly mannered, the purity of the angel lost to a certain self-satisfied air which renders it slightly comical and aspiritual. Humanism is taken to its extreme, so much so that there is little room left in the painting for the superhuman experience to unfold.

△ **A Raft of Cherubs** *(detail)*
Danti, Egnazio (1536-86)

THIS DETAIL IS taken from the Gallery of Maps, in Rome, commissioned by Pope Gregory XIII between 1580-83. It is unusual to see angels appearing in a cartographer's art, but nevertheless here is evidence of one rare Renaissance occasion. The map is held in the Vatican and perhaps the inclusion of spirits offered it a necessary religiosity. It is probably more likely that, by the time of the map's creation, cherubs had become little more than decorative and popular icons in Roman culture and were included, along with a mermaid, to add life and vitality to the scene, bringing messages of human kind from foreign climes. They certainly succeed.

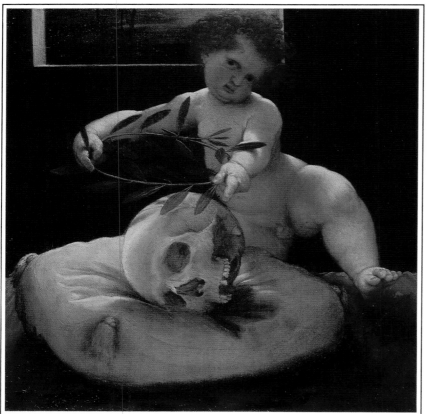

◁ **Cherub with a Skull**
Lorenzo Lotto (1480-1556)

THIS IS AN unusual composition, but its horizontal position is common to Lotto. An eclectic artist, he never established a striking personal style, but in this example the artist has succeed in creating a chilling and thought-provoking image. The cherub ironically places a 'crown' around the skull of a dead man. His face holds a discreet and unsettling expression, this cherub is one whom we may not feel we could trust upon meeting. He is perhaps a messenger of Azrael, the Angel of Death, bringing to earth the message of mortality.

▷ **The Isenheim Altarpiece**
(detail)
Mathis Grünewald (1470/80-
1528)

THERE ARE FEW religious works
revered so much as this
altarpiece, from which this detail
of the Angel Gabriel is taken.
Grünewald was a high Gothic
artist who had an understanding
of Renaissance classicism and the
laws of perspective, yet chose to
imbue his paintings with intense
emotion and colours more in
keeping with his northern roots.
Gabriel here is a glorious yet
imposing figure, talking
emphatically to the Madonna,
passing on God's message of the
immaculate conception. His hair
is the colour of saffron, as
tradition decreed, and he is
depicted with an intense
humanism. The book Mary
holds open on her knee is likely to
be Isaiah, Chapter 29, verses
eleven and twelve, which contain
the words: 'behold, a virgin
shall conceive'.

▷ **The Ascension of Christ**
Jacopo Tintoretto (1518-94)

THE RADICAL, anti-Classical style
developed by Tintoretto in Venice
during the 16th century marked a
turning point in High Renaissance
art. Tintoretto stole the limelight
from the school of Titian with his
rejection of naturalism in
exchange for the drama of
expressionism – through which
Mannerism was born. This fresco
was painted late in his career,
1576-81. It was the last of ten wall
paintings which decorated the
ceiling of the Sculoa di San
Rocco, Venice. The angels' wings
create repetitive rhythms and
spatial dynamism. They frame the
figures of Christ and the disciples
as a picture within a picture, a
dramatic encounter between the
spiritual world of angels and the
physical one of humanity.

▷ **Putto with a Red Flower**
Paolo Veronese (1528-88)

HERE WE SEE a putto (cherub) of classical nature – a Renaissance device to which we still assume accuracy today. Veronese was a Venetian who chose to follow Titian in preference to the new Mannerism of Tintoretto. The cherub is nature incarnate: fresh-fleshed and curly-haired, softly curving around the scene. The form is fluent and appealing, but there is little evidence of emotion for the viewer to share in.

Detail

▷ **Madonna Carried by Angels**
Jacopo Palma (Il Giovane) (1544-1628)

PALMA MAY HAVE been invigorated
by the colours and Classical forms
of Titian, but this prolific Venetian
was a Mannerist in mood and
composition. The marriage of the
two schools within this ceiling
fresco creates a beguiling image.
The Madonna is a vision of
serenity itself, yet her impassive
features contrast with the drama
of the scene enveloping her. The
cherubs lift her on high, creating a
repetitive and decorative motif
which raises her towards heaven.
The light source appears to
emanate from behind, yet the
Madonna's face is illuminated,
in dramatic contrast to her dark
and billowing robes, within which
float the cherubs.

Detail

▷ **The Annunciation**
Peter Paul Rubens (1577-1640)

THE UNDEBATED master of
Northern Baroque, Rubens
honed his skills as a young painter
in Italy. High drama imbues this
Annunciation scene. Note how
Gabriel's golden locks catch the
light, how the Madonna's hand
lies poised to turn the page of her
scriptures. The detailed execution
includes the carving of an angel
in the piece of furniture by which
she stands, denoting human
adulation of the spiritual life.
Cherubs, which adorn the ceiling,
emphasize the heavenly nature of
Gabriel's visitation and also
confirm the influence upon
Rubens of Carravaggio and other
Renaissance masters.

Detail

▷ **Annunciation**
El Greco (Domenikos Theotocopoulos) (1541-1614)

EL GRECO'S religious vision adorns churches and monasteries throughout the medieval Spanish city of Toledo. His use of lime greens and cerulean blues, sharp pinks and lemon yellows retain their vibrance on his frescoes even today. High drama, light and colour denote a rejection of the Classical and confirm his early Venetian training in the Mannerist style. Note how Gabriel's limbs are elongated to express weightlessness, how elaborate the composition has become, how the actual story of the Annunciation is almost secondary to the climactic nature of the experience, emphasized by the cherubs who serve no narrative purpose yet proliferate, drawing our eyes upwards towards the angelic choir, making their spiritually uplifting music on high. Rhythm percolates down and into the forms of the main figures beneath, where Gabriel is gowned simply in green to contrast with the Titianesque crimson of Mary's shining robes.

◁ **Flight Into Egypt**
Michelangelo Carravaggio
(1573-1610)

THIS UNUSUAL IMAGE shows the back of an angel playing a violin to Joseph's music, allowing the viewer a splendid view of his wings. These, in their realistic depiction, are closer in their association to birds than spirits. Carravaggio, Leonardo da Vinci and Botticelli all used birds such as geese, swans and eagles as reference in their painting of angels' wings. Carravaggio was much criticized during his lifetime for his vivid realism, for not idealizing religious subjects. As here, he clothed the figures in contemporary peasant dress. He did not create the Virgin and Child as goddess and little prince, but rather as mother and son, fatigued from their enforced flight out of Bethlehem after Herod had ordered the murder of all infant boys under the age of two. The angel is unrobed, other than for his classical drapes, and has more the appearance of a young shepherd boy than a messenger from God. He probably represents Gabriel. The chiaroscuro effects of starkly contrasting light and dark are characteristic of Carravaggio's style, in which beauty and truth in nature were the fundamental objectives.

△ **Two Flying Cherubs Holding the Crown of Thorns and the Spear of Longimus**
Andrea Podesta Giovanni (1620-74)

IN THIS BAROQUE painting of cherubs, Giovanni depicts them removing two symbols of man's lack of faith in Christ. The crown of thorns was placed on Christ's head in mockery by Pilate's soldiers. St Longimus was the soldier in the gospel of St John who wounded Christ in his side with a spear. He was said to be blind, and, after the event, upon rubbing his eyes with his blood-smeared hands, he regained his vision.

Detail

◁ **The Assumption of Mary Magdalene**
José Antolinez (1635-75)

TYPICALLY flamboyant in style, the bright blues and strong lighting make Mary's assumption both theatrical and regal. The cherubs are carrying Mary's body and soul to God – note Uriel, with his musical instrument providing her with a sweet tune to accompany her on her journey.

Detail

▷ **The Holy Family**
Hermensz van Rijn Rembrandt (1606-69)

Oil on canvas

THIS SCENE SHOWS the Holy Family as lowly subjects, Mary sits cradling Jesus while Joseph chops wood. The figures are in no way glorified but the whole scene is imbued with Rembrandt's golden light. The cherubs, watching over the Madonna and Child, add a spiritual dimension to an otherwise sombre scene. Their heavenly glow links the simple family to the celestial world from which they come.

Detail

◁ **Christ Supported by Angels**
Francesco Trevisani (1656-1746)

TREVISANI WAS born in Naples
and active in Rome from 1678.
In this highly theatrical Baroque
painting, the paradox of agony
and ecstasy in Christ's death is
painstakingly portrayed. The
image holds an overwhelming
emotional appeal, with strong
chiaroscuro, balance and
harmony. The two idyllic child
angels wear one blue, one red
gown – linking them to the
traditional symbols of cherubim
and seraphim who have blue and
red wings, respectively.

◁ **Angels and Doves**
François Boucher (1703-70)

Oil on canvas

BOUCHER IS ONE of the most celebrated of Rococo artists – a famous painter of baby cherubs. He relished exuberance, sensuality and artificiality in his paintings, striving to achieve the impression of an idealized, perfect world. The wings of the cherubs are as soft and downy as the feathers on the doves, their skin as pink and fresh as a newborn baby's – yet they have adult, characterful faces. Innocence is mixed with adult knowledge in this provocatively sensual scene.

▷ **The Annunciation**
c 1757-62
Giovanni-Battista Tiepolo (1696-1770)

Fresco

UNLIKE HIS MORE Rococo paintings, Tiepolo's pen and ink drawing is simplicity itself. It is a spiritually uplifting image of Gabriel, gesturing heavenward to Mary, whose figure is hunched in humility, her head covered by a scarf. This drawing is all light and line, and offers an unadorned view of the Annunciation.

◁ **The Agony in the Garden**
Francisco Jose de Goya
y Lucientes (1746-1828)

Oil on canvas

PAINTED LATE IN Goya's life, after
serious illness, this picture shows
all the signs of the artist's own
horrific nightmares and visions.
Christ's eyes are wide and white,
almost unseeing. The angel is
holding the cup of salvation from
which the guilty must drink before
being allowed to ascend to heaven.
Rather than the three disciples
who are said to have accompanied
Jesus to the garden of
Gethsemane, Jesus has only one
companion: a faithful dog.

△ **Cupid on Guard**
Thomas Stothard (1755-1834)

Oil on canvas

THE LEOPARD IS the symbol of sin and destruction, as we can learn from the words in the Book of Revelations: 'And the beast I saw was like unto a leopard'. Chammel, the Duke of Hell, was also sometimes portrayed as a leopard. He was the ruler of Mars, the evil planet of war. Cupid is seen here, as a cherub, entertaining Mars.

Detail

▷ **Christ in the Sepulchre, Guarded by Angels**
William Blake (1757-1827)

CHRIST IS enshrined in the same cloth which robes the angels, linking his mortal body to their spiritual life. Blake often painted angels and exploited the shape of their wings to create highly decorative scenes. The painting is simple, beautiful and mystical, the light which permeates between the parallel wings of the angels symbolizing Christ's ascension. One angel is male, one female, and their earthly, naked forms are perceptible beneath the pale muslin cloth.

Detail

◁ **Madonna Wrapping the Christ Child in Swaddling Clothes**
Bartoleme Esteban Murillo (1617-82)

Oil on canvas

MURILLO WAS BORN and lived in Seville. He was a realist in his depiction of figures, but was greatly influenced by the northern Baroque. There is genuine warmth and sensitivity in this portrayal of the Madonna and child, and they have distinctly human features – as do the two musical angels playing to them. This is an emotive scene in which the cherubs, who are winged but have no bodies, crown the Madonna and emanate a heavenly light.

Detail

▷ **Swarms of Cherubs, a Group of Children in the Sky**
Jean-Honoré Fragonard (1732-1806)

Oil on canvas

FRAGONARD'S CHERUBS are in competition with Boucher's for their sickly sweetness. In fact, Fragonard studied under Boucher and was another exponent of the French Rococo style. Anti-realism rules on high. The cherubs dominate the sky, tumbling softly through the clouds like balls of pink and white cotton wool in a lady's toilette. They are ornaments with little religious significance, and the picture's title, equating cherubs with children, denotes the fine line which Fragonard has happily crossed between religious symbolism and a purely decorative art.

Detail

▷ **Ecce Ancillia Domini, The Annunciation**
Dante Gabriel Rossetti (1828-82)

Oil on canvas

IN THIS MODERN portrayal, Gabriel appears floating on a golden cloud appealing to the Madonna – the epitome of medieval beauty with her long red hair, tinted white skin, deep set eyes and blood-red lips. As Christina Rossetti said of her brother's paintings:

> *One face looks out from all his*
> *canvases...*
> *One self-same figure sits, or walks*
> *or leans,*
> *Not as she is, but as she fills his*
> *dreams.*

The Pre-Raphaelites strove to portray the ideal of medieval beauty on the canvas. The image is based on Rossetti's wife, Elizabeth Siddal. The Madonna is innocent yet sensual, Gabriel is unwinged, although he has a halo, and he appears to Mary in her bed-chamber at the moment of conception.

▷ **The Dream of St Cecilia**
Paul Baudry (1826-86)

Oil on canvas

ST CECILIA was forced to marry
but she made her husband vow to
respect her chastity. If he did not,
she warned him, the angel who
watched over her would punish
him. St Cecilia's Day is a
celebration of music, hence all of
the angels who appear here
carry musical instruments. This
Baroque painting makes full use of
spatial dimensions and the angels
are garbed in classical robes.
The image is full of drama
and emotion.

△ **The Angel Musician**
Edward Burne-Jones (1833-98)

Stained glass (for William Morris & Co)

THE PRE-RAPHAELITE and Arts
and Crafts Movements worked
hand in hand, and this stained
glass window was commissioned
by the latter, in the form of
William Morris & Company, to a
member of the former. It is a
dreamy, romantic image, showing
the influence of Mantegna and
Botticelli on Burne-Jones. He was
more influenced by Renaissance
art than his friend Rossetti, and
was interested in representing
images through flat colour and
simplified form. The Angel of
Music is probably Uriel. Here,
his finely drawn face and musical
instrument contrast with the
decorative red glass of his robes
and wings, and the repeated
pattern of flowers which
provide a background.

◁ **The Ramparts of God's House**
John Melhuish Stradwick
(1849-1937)

Oil and gold leaf on canvas

THIS IMAGE IS steeped in romantic medievalism, the angels garbed in gold and silver, their wings large and finely detailed, their halos shining. The paint surface is richly encrusted. Stradwick was one of the last upholders of the Pre-Raphaelite tradition. His figures are characteristically tall and slender and the elaborate style is particular to him. The angels are Pre-Raphaelite maidens – very much female figures rather than celestial beings. Their clothes are so classical that they could almost be carved from stone, as are replicas of them in the ramparts. The building in which they reside is so heavily influenced by the Arts and Crafts movement that it could have been designed by William Morris. Angels fill every nook and cranny, as befits the House of God.

◁ **Angel Traveller**
Gustave Moreau (1826-96)

Oil on canvas

GUSTAVE MOREAU painted many
religious scenes and allegories in a
highly elaborate, finely detailed
style. The leader of the Symbolist
movement, he impasted his oil
onto the canvas until the surface
was encrusted with paint. This is a
fine example, the angel is
elaborately executed, with long,
elegant wings and gold threads
woven in his robes. His figure is
boyish yet refined, and he hangs
his head and closes his wings in
fatigue as he rests on a Cathedral
wall, looking down over a wide
open, simplistically painted
cityscape, where spires rise
heavenward. The muted tones
contrast with the angel's vivid
attire, emphasizing his remoteness
from the human world.

△ Jacob Wrestling with the Angel – The Vision after the Sermon
Paul Gauguin (1848-1903)

Oil on canvas

PAINTED IN 1888, this is the pictorial embodiment of Synthetism, Gauguin's theory of using flat, bold colours to symbolize the forces of nature. The painting combines Breton peasant life with religious allegory. The red ground highlights the visionary and imagined nature of the scene set before the peasant women. Gauguin wrote to Vincent van Gogh in 1888 that: 'The landscape and the fight exist only in the imagination of the people at prayer after a sermon.'

This story has also been represented by Delacroix (1857-60). Jacob wrestled throughout the night with an unknown angel by the side of a ford. In the morning, the angel touched the hollow in Jacob's thigh and told him that he would bless him and that his name would no longer be Jacob but Israel. The wrestling match has been seen as a fight between Jacob and God, or Jacob and his conscience. The angel is thought to have been Uriel, who is also known as the Face or Fire of God.

Detail

◁ **Angel**
Abbott Handerson Thayer
(1849-1921)

Oil on canvas

A BEAUTIFUL STUDY in 19th
century American realism,
Thayer's angel is depicted as a
young girl dressed in the colour of
ivory, with ivory-coloured wings
which frame the image like folds
of fabric. Her cheeks are slightly
rose-tinted, hinting at a sexual
awakening, yet she retains purity
and chastity still.

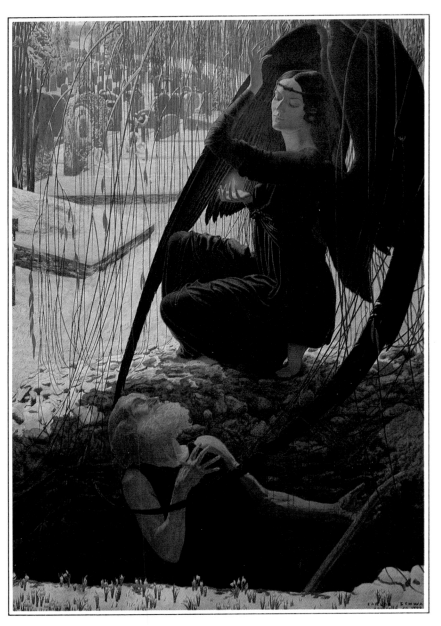

◁ **The Angel of Death**
Carlos Schwabe (1866-1926)

Oil on canvas

THIS IS A vainglorious image of the
Angel of Death enfolding man
under her wings, ready to escort
him to the kingdom of Heaven.
She is a classical image of beauty,
with her gorgeous jade dress and
long, fine fingers the epitome of
elegance and refinement. She
entices her subject out of his grave
to follow her. She is ever-young
and imbues a cool, green light
against the chill white snow
settling in the cemetery around
her. This is a realist Victorian
image in which Azrael, the Angel
of Death, is in control of man's
destiny. In mythology she sits on
the throne in the sixth heaven,
covered in eyes, and it is said that
when one closes, an angel dies.

△ **An Angel**
Marc Chagall (1887-1985)

Stained glass

MANY OF CHAGALL'S paintings, drawings and stained glass windows contain subjects floating in the air – people, cows, candelabra – and sometimes angels. In this simple church window the angel's figure is simplified and, to a degree, abstracted. The angel lacks elegance, and appears more like a young boy than a celestial body. Chagall uses the colours of his painting palette in his choice of glass – blues, greens and pinks.

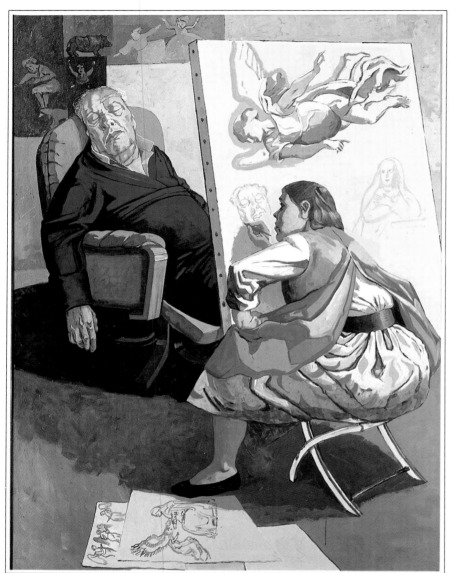

◁ **Joseph's Dream** 1990
Paula Rego (born 1935)

Acrylic on paper laid on canvas

JOSEPH, IN THE BOOK of Genesis, was said to have had two dreams which foretold of his superiority over his two brothers. Paula Rego painted her version of the dreams while resident artist at the National Gallery in London in 1990. It shows a version of Philippe de Champaigne's painting of Saint Joseph which hangs in the gallery. Rego's work is the final one in a sequence called *Time – Past and Present*. The little girl of the earlier works has now grown into an adult woman whose comely figure sits precariously on the stool as she draws angels of Joseph's dreams.

This is a modern painting and its religious imagery is used by Rego as a visual device to tell a secular story. It is a picture within a picture of another picture and Rego is the artist both inside and outside of the frame.

ACKNOWLEDGEMENTS

The Publisher would like to thank the following for their kind permission to reproduce the paintings in this book:

Bridgeman Art Library, London /Museo Diocesano de Solsona, Lerida/Index: 8; **/Scrovegni (Arena) Chapel, Padua:** 9; **/Museo di San Marco dell'Angelico, Florence:** 10; **/Bibliotheque Nationale, Paris:** 11; **/Hotel Dieu, Beaune:** 12-13; **/Louvre, Paris:** 14-15; **/Galleria degli Uffizi, Florence:** 16-17, 22-23, 30-32; **/Galleria dell'Accademia, Florence:** 18-19, 28-29; **/Accademia di San Luca, Rome/K & B News Foto, Florence:** 20; **/Staatliche Kunstsammlungen, Dresden:** 21; **/Prado, Madrid:** 24-25, 34-35, 46-47, 50-51; **/Museo Correr, Venice:** 26; **/Pushkin Museum, Moscow:** 27; **/National Gallery, London:** 33; **/Fitzwilliam Museum, University of Cambridge:** 36; **/Vatican Museums & Galleries, Rome:** 37; **/Private Collection:** 38; **/Unterlinden Museum, Colmar, France:** 39; **/Scuola Grande di San Rocco, Venice:** 40; **/The Trustees of the Weston Park Foundation:** 41; **/Oratorio dei Crociferi, Venice:** 42-43; **/Kunsthisorisches Museum, Vienna:** 44-45; **/Palazzo Doria Pamphili, Rome:** 48; **/Phillips, The International Fine Art Auctioneers:** 49; **/Hermitage, St Petersburg:** 52-53; **/City of Bristol Museum & Art Gallery:** 54-55; **/Rafael Valls Gallery, London:** 56; **/Courtauld Institute Galleries, University of London:** 57; **/Christie's, London:** 58, 70-71; **/Simon Carter Gallery, Woodbridge:** 59; **/Victoria & Albert Museum, London:** 60-61; **/Museum of Fine Arts, Budapest:** 62-63; **/Louvre, Paris/Giraudon:** 64-65; **/Tate Gallery, London:** 66-67; **/Church of St Peter & St Paul, Cattistock, Dorset:** 68; **/Musee des Beaux-Arts, Moulins/Giraudon:** 69; **/Palais de Tokyo, Paris:** 72; **/Musee Gustave Moreau, Paris:** 74; **/National Gallery of Scotland, Edinburgh:** 75; **/National Museum of American Art, Smithsonian Inst., Washington DC/Art Resource, New York:** Cover, Half-title, 76; **/All Saints, Tudeley, Kent:** 77 **Private Collection. Photo: Marlborough Fine Art (London) Ltd:** 78